# Table of Contents

D0861066

# Let Newton Be!

Imagine a world where nobody knows why the Earth goes round the sun. Imagine that they don't know why things fall downward when dropped. Imagine a world without cars, television, or computers. That was the world before Isaac Newton.

Isaac Newton

Newton was born and grew up in the countryside.

# Isaac Newton
## and the
# Laws of the Universe

Jane Weir, MPhys

# Physical Science Readers:
# Isaac Newton and the Laws of the Universe

## Publishing Credits

**Editorial Director**
Dona Herweck Rice

**Creative Director**
Lee Aucoin

**Associate Editor**
Joshua BishopRoby

**Illustration Manager**
Timothy J. Bradley

**Editor-in-Chief**
Sharon Coan, M.S.Ed.

**Publisher**
Rachelle Cracchiolo, M.S.Ed.

**Science Contributor**
Sally Ride Science

**Science Consultants**
Michael E. Kopecky,
    Science Department Chair,
    Chino Hills High School
Jane Weir, MPhys

## *Teacher Created Materials*

5301 Oceanus Drive
Huntington Beach, CA 92649-1030
http://www.tcmpub.com
ISBN 978-0-7439-0574-9
© 2007 Teacher Created Materials, Inc.
Reprinted 2012

On January 4, 1643, Isaac Newton was born in Lincolnshire, England. He arrived much too early and was very small. No one thought he would live. But he did. His mother said he was so small he could fit inside a quart mug.

Newton's father was a farmer. He died a few months before his son was born. When Newton was two years old, his mother remarried. She went to live with her new husband. She did not take her young son with her. Newton's stepfather would not let her take him. She left her son in the care of his grandmother. She and her new husband had three more children.

Newton was without his mother until the age of ten. At that time, his stepfather died. His mother and her children came home to be with Newton.

### Birthday

Newton's birthday is January 4, 1643, if using the calendar we use today. But in Newton's time, a different calendar was used. According to that calendar, he was born on December 25, 1642, which is Christmas Day.

Newton went to the neighborhood school. At first he didn't do well. The teachers said he didn't pay attention. He was then sent to a bigger and better grammar school. It was called The King's School. He carved his name on the windowsill in the school library. People can still see it there today.

He became the best student at King's. They called this honor "top boy." While at this school, he lived with a local family. He became engaged to their daughter. When Newton left there for college, he focused on his studies. He didn't pay much attention to the girl back home. She married someone else. Newton never married anyone. People say that he always had warm feelings for his first love.

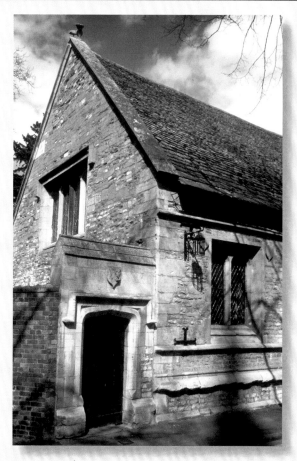

Newton's boyhood school still stands.

Statue of Aristotle

Newton's mother wanted him to be a farmer. He tried to please her. He tried farming before he tried college. But he couldn't stop thinking about his studies. He wasn't happy as a farmer. The head of King's school convinced his mother to send him to college.

The students in college studied Aristotle (AIR-uh-stot-uhl). He was a Greek philosopher from long ago. Newton wanted to study newer and better ideas. He took it upon himself to learn about modern philosophers and scientists.

## Master of the Mint

In his later life, Newton was in charge of the Royal Mint. His job was to replace the old hand-made coins with new ones made by machines. He was also in charge of finding people who made fake money.

## Absent-Minded Mathematician

Newton was absent-minded. Legend has it that Newton, when holding parties, would wander off to get refreshments for his guests but start working out a math problem instead. He would forget to go back to dinner!

The legend of Newton being hit on the head with an apple is how many people remember him.

*Nature and nature's laws lay hid in night:*
*God said, "Let Newton be!" and all was light.*

Alexander Pope, the famous English writer, said this about Newton. He meant that Newton was able to explain mysteries of nature that nobody else could.

In order to help his studies, Newton invented a new math. It was called **calculus** (KAL-kyuh-luhs). But he didn't like to talk about himself or his work. He didn't tell anyone about his new math for 30 years.

⬆ Alexander Pope

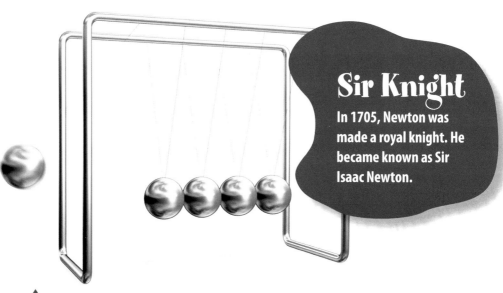

## Sir Knight

In 1705, Newton was made a royal knight. He became known as Sir Isaac Newton.

⬆ This toy is called a Newton's Cradle. It illustrates some of Newton's discoveries about motion.

Newton was very good at using math to describe things that he saw happen in nature. Motion is one of these things. Motion is caused by **force**. Newton did not know what caused the forces of nature. But he knew he could measure their effects, such as motion. This is what he spent most of his life working on.

The measurement of forces are required to send a rocket into space.

# Laura Bassi (1711-1778)

Laura Bassi was one of the first women ever to earn a doctorate (DOK-ter-it) degree. That is the highest degree a person can earn. She was also one of the first to become a paid professor at a university. In school, she studied all types of science and math. She also learned four languages. Bassi married a fellow teacher. They had 12 children. She continued to work while she raised her children. She fought to be given greater responsibility at the university. She also fought for better pay and better equipment to do experiments in physics. She was one of the first scientists to study and follow the teachings of Newton.

# Newton's Ideas

## Principia

Newton wrote a famous book about forces and the way things move. This book has a long name in Latin. It is called the *Principia* for short. It is one of the most important scientific books ever written.

Newton didn't like showing off his work. He only published his book because his friends urged him. One friend even paid for it to be published.

Newton's *Principia*, published in 1687

The book has three parts. The first part is about gravity. Newton shows that gravity makes everything that has **mass** attract everything else. The second part is about how things move in substances such as air and water. The third part is about the motion of planets and other bodies in space.

## Newtonian Mechanics

Newton described forces so well that the math used now to figure how things move is named after him. It is called Newtonian Mechanics. Using this math, we can map the path of a strawberry as it falls through the air into a bowl. We can work out how fast a stone will fall after it is dropped. We can figure out how much effort is needed to pick up a book. We can explain the moon's path around Earth. In fact, the movement of anything we see can be explained with Newton's system.

### A Dark Force?

Philosophers in Newton's time criticized his theory of gravity because he didn't explain what caused it. They thought it made gravity sound like a mysterious, dark force. That frightened them. Newton refused to guess at what gravity actually is. He just stuck to describing the way it moves things.

### The Newton

The standard international (SI) unit used to measure force is the **newton**, named after Isaac Newton.

The strawberries falling portray gravity, which was explained in Newton's first law. The strawberries displacing the milk portray Newton's second law.

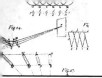

# Laws of Motion

Newton is perhaps most famous for three laws about the way things move. Newton didn't write the laws. Other scientists studying his work wrote them. They called them Newton's Laws of Motion. Newtonian Mechanics is based on the Laws of Motion.

## Newton's First Law

Newton's First Law of Motion is the law of **inertia** (in-UR-shuh). Inertia means resistance to changes in motion. The law says that an object will keep doing what it's doing so long as an unbalanced force doesn't act on it. This works for things that are still and for things that are moving. Things that are still will stay still. Things that are moving will keep moving in a straight line with the same speed.

According to Newton's First Law, a bicycle won't change its motion until something makes it change.

# Newton's Second Law

Newton's Second Law is the law of **acceleration**. It describes what happens when you apply a force to an object. It says that the bigger the force, the more the object speeds up or slows down. It also says that the object will always move in the same direction of the force. A bigger force is needed to make a heavier object speed up or slow down by the same amount as a light object. This makes sense. For example, a bowling ball is harder to throw than a tennis ball. It is harder to stop a car than a bicycle.

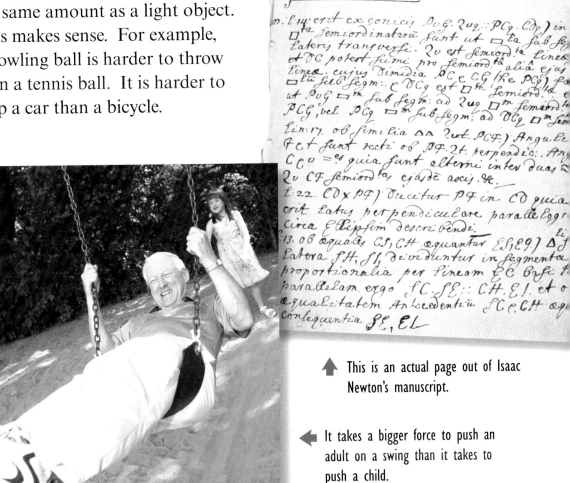

▲ This is an actual page out of Isaac Newton's manuscript.

◀ It takes a bigger force to push an adult on a swing than it takes to push a child.

## Newton's Third Law

Newton's Third Law of Motion is the law of action and reaction. For every action, there is an equal and opposite reaction. So whenever a force pushes on an object, the object pushes back in the opposite direction. The force of the object pushing back is called the reaction force.

This law explains many things. For example, it explains why we can move a rowboat in water with an oar. The water pushes back on the oar as much as the oar pushes on the water. This moves the boat. It also explains why a chair stays where it is instead of crashing through the floor. The floor pushes back and keeps it there. Also, when you hit a baseball with a bat, the ball pushes on the bat as much as the bat pushes on the ball. Hit it just right, and all that force creates a home run!

## Fun in Motion

They may or may not know it, but snowboarders use forces and motion to perform stunts. As a snowboarder travels downhill, she picks up speed because she is being accelerated by gravity. The reaction force of the slope pushes her away from the slope and forward. Friction and air resistance both oppose her motion and act to slow her down. She can use wax on the base of her board to reduce friction between the board and snow and to make her go faster. She can tuck down to reduce drag, which speeds her up, too. When she tips the board to one side, she changes the direction the reaction force is acting in. This makes her turn. As she pulls an ollie (a type of jump on the board), she can bend, twist, and lean to change the center of gravity of her body on the board and keep herself steady.

The force of the ball on the bat as it is hit is called the reaction force. It is created in reaction to the force made by the swinging bat.

Imagine trying to throw a snowball without gravity. If you threw the snowball in the air, then it would just disappear into space and never come back!

## Gravity

Newton realized that the force that makes planets go around the sun is the same force that makes things fall to Earth. It is called **gravity** (GRAV-i-tee). A story about Newton says that he figured out gravity when he saw an apple fall from a tree. He realized that the apple and the moon are similar. Gravity attracts them both to Earth.

Gravity is what holds us on the ground. It keeps us from floating into space. It also keeps Earth going around the sun. And it keeps the moon going around Earth. Without gravity, things would just bob in space.

Newton watched the planets in the sky. He figured out that the planets were pulled towards the sun. The closer the planets were to the sun, the stronger the pull on them.

## Escape!

If you can make something go fast enough, it will have enough energy to escape Earth's gravity and go into orbit. Earth's **escape velocity** is 11 kilometers (7 miles) per second, which is very fast. This is how space vehicles are able to leave Earth.

# Emilie de Breteuil

## (1706-1749)

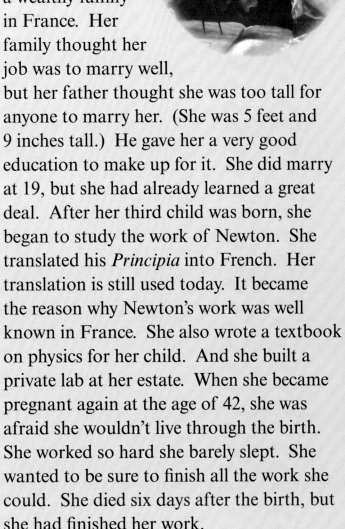

De Breteuil was born into a wealthy family in France. Her family thought her job was to marry well, but her father thought she was too tall for anyone to marry her. (She was 5 feet and 9 inches tall.) He gave her a very good education to make up for it. She did marry at 19, but she had already learned a great deal. After her third child was born, she began to study the work of Newton. She translated his *Principia* into French. Her translation is still used today. It became the reason why Newton's work was well known in France. She also wrote a textbook on physics for her child. And she built a private lab at her estate. When she became pregnant again at the age of 42, she was afraid she wouldn't live through the birth. She worked so hard she barely slept. She wanted to be sure to finish all the work she could. She died six days after the birth, but she had finished her work.

He also watched the moon. He learned that the moon was pulled towards the Earth. If Earth's gravity stopped pulling on it, the moon would head off in a straight line away from Earth. This is Newton's first law. Earth's gravity gives it a constant tug. This pulls it around in a circle. Think of a ball on a string. If you swing the ball around your head, then the tension in the string acts like gravity. It keeps the ball moving in a circle. The ball would fly off at an angle if you were to let go of the string. This is what would happen to the moon if Earth's gravity stopped working.

The moon has energy from its motion. That is why Earth's gravity doesn't make the moon fall down and land on Earth. If something came along that stopped the moon from moving, then it would start falling toward Earth. Just as in the ball example, if you let the ball slow down too much, then it will collapse toward you!

Gravity keeps the moon from pulling away from Earth, just as this string keeps the ball in motion from being thrown away from the post.

Moon

Earth

# Why Does a Roller Coaster Make Your Tummy Go Funny?

When you jump off something high or go down a steep slope on a roller coaster, you are under the influence of gravity. You feel weightless when this happens because there is no reaction force pressing up under you. In a roller coaster, gravity is acting on your seat and accelerating (ak-SEL-uh-rate-ing) it downward at the same rate as you. That's why it doesn't push upward with a reaction force like a seat usually does. Your insides can move about, but the inside of your body is made mostly of water, so there is more **drag** there than outside. This stops some of your internal organs from being accelerated as fast as the outside of your body at first. So, you feel a jolt (like your stomach coming up into your mouth) until the outside of your body catches up with your insides and forces them to accelerate with the rest of your body!

## Light

Newton disagreed with the theories of his time about light. People thought that **white light** was natural light. They thought that colored light was made when light went through air or water and was changed. They thought that a rainbow (called a **spectrum**) comes from a **prism** (PRIZ-uhm) because the prism changes the light.

Newton did an experiment with two glass prisms. He showed that, if the spectrum coming from one prism was put through another prism, the colors didn't change again. So he knew that white light must be made of all the colors of the rainbow. It was just broken up into different colors through the prism. From this, people could explain why rainbows happen.

Newton changed people's understanding of light. But many people criticized his ideas. He got tired of defending them. So he didn't publish his work on light until 30 years after he completed it.

White light is composed of all the colors in the rainbow at once. A prism separates the different colors in white light so you can see them individually.

## Humble Scientist

Newton was modest about his achievements. He once said that, if he had seen further than other people, it was because he had stood on the shoulders of giants. This meant that he recognized that his discoveries had their roots in the ideas of scientists who had gone before him.

Newton invented many gadgets. Some of them are still used today. He invented a **reflecting microscope** (MY-kruh-skope). He designed and built the first **reflector telescope** (TEL-uh-skope). They both use mirrors. Before this, all telescopes used lenses. Lenses are curved pieces of glass such as those used in eyeglasses. The type of telescope that Newton invented is still used. It is very good for looking at groups of stars. It is called the Newtonian telescope.

Quality lenses were important to Newton. He decided to play with lenses and a glass plate to see what he could figure out. He showed that shining a light on the lens and plate at a certain angle could produce rings of light. We call these **Newton's Rings**. They are used for testing the quality of lens surfaces.

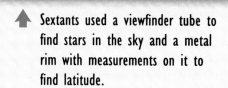

Sextants used a viewfinder tube to find stars in the sky and a metal rim with measurements on it to find latitude.

Newton's Rings ➡

Newton also wrote a formula to describe how far away a lens will focus light. This is called the lens equation. It is useful for making anything with a lens in it. In fact, Newton ground his own lenses for his telescopes.

Sailors of his time owed thanks to Newton. He designed the **sextant**. The sextant helped sailors to find their position at sea. They used the sun and stars to do it.

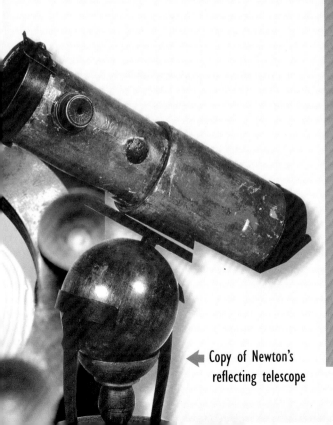

← Copy of Newton's reflecting telescope

## Newton's Chicken

Newton is such a famous and important scientist that everyone knows about him. He's so well-known that people even tell jokes about him. Here are some answers to a famous joke that tell about Newton's laws of motion and gravity.

*Why did the chicken cross the road?*
**First Law of Motion:** Chickens at rest stay at rest. Chickens in motion cross the road.

**Second Law of Motion:** The chicken was pushed.

**Third Law of Motion:** The chicken was pushed by another chicken who knocked itself over by pushing so hard.

Law of Gravity: The chicken was attracted to a bigger chicken waiting across the road.

## Secret Solver

In 1662, the Royal Society was set up in England. This was like a "clever scientists club." It supported research and discovery in science. Scientists met and talked about things that puzzled them. Sometimes they gave a problem to one another as a challenge. Newton was very good at solving their problems.

In 1696, a Swiss **mathematician** (math-uh-muh-TISH-uhn) gave a problem for all the math experts of Europe to solve. He gave them six months to do it. Newton solved it in a single night. He didn't like discussing his math proofs, so he published the answer anonymously in a Royal Society magazine. (In fact, Newton didn't publish any of his math texts under his own name until he was 60 years old.)

When another famous scientist gave another problem, Newton solved it in a single night, too. These were just two of many difficult math problems he solved. In 1703, Newton was made president of the Royal Society.

## A New Branch of Math

Newton invented a way of using math to go back and forth between things that are related, like surface area and volume, or speed and acceleration. His method is now called calculus. It is a whole branch of math. Newton also wrote a rule called the **binomial theorem**. It is used to solve math problems.

## End of His Work

Newton worked on new ideas and inventions until he died on March 20, 1727. He was 85 years old. He lived a full and rich life. When he died, many people mourned his loss. He was buried at Westminster Abbey with much pomp and ceremony. Many famous and important people from England are buried there.

# Civil Engineer: Oksana Wall

**Walt Disney World®**

## Riding High

When Oksana Wall was 13, she and her family came from Venezuela to visit Walt Disney World®. She wondered who created the rides. When she found out they were designed by engineers, she decided she wanted to become an engineer, too. For Disney, of course.

Now Wall works on all kinds of rides, making sure they are fun, safe, and unique. "I really love working on many projects," she says. "I have a blast at my job."

The best part for Wall? "We get to enjoy the attractions ourselves, and we get to see our guests enjoy them too." Who are the "guests"? That's you.

## Being There

Designing a ride requires the teamwork and cooperation of mechanical engineers, electrical engineers, architects, and artists.

## Experts Tell Us . . .

"What makes a good ride is when you enjoy the fantasy, and you escape reality."

◀ Wall's job is to think up new ideas for thrilling roller coasters and other rides.

Satisfied riders get to feel ▶
all of Newton's laws on
Wall's coasters.

## Materials

- stopwatch
- a piece of string 1.25 meters long
- 50 grams of play clay (plasticine)
- a laboratory stand and clamp, or sticky tape and a table or door frame
- sheet of paper
- marker

## Procedure

1 Cut a piece of string to 1.25 meters.

2 Make a pendulum by molding a lump of plasticine onto the end of the piece of string.

3 Measure 1 meter up the string from the center of the plasticine blob. Put a mark on the string. Tie it to the stand and clamp it at the 1-meter mark. If you are doing this at home and don't have a stand and clamp, then you can tape the pendulum to a table edge or door frame.

4    Hold the pendulum blob to one side. Get ready with the stopwatch.

5    Let go of the pendulum and start the stopwatch.

6    Count 10 full swings (stopping point and back) of your pendulum. Then, stop the stopwatch when it arrives back at the start for the tenth time.

7    Record the time the pendulum took to make 10 swings.

8    Shorten your pendulum to .5 meters and repeat the experiment.

9    Figure out the time in seconds for one swing by dividing the time for 10 swings by 10. This is called the period of the pendulum.

10    Record your results in a table like the one shown here.

11    With the period you calculated (the time for one swing of the pendulum) in Step 9, find the force of gravity. You will use this formula:

gravity = (39 x length) / (swing time x swing time)

Calculate the gravity for each of the two pendula you made. It's tricky, but you can do it!

How do the values for gravity compare? What effect does changing the length of the pendulum have on the period?

**10**

| Pendulum Length | Time for 10 Swings | Time for 1 Swing |
|---|---|---|
| 1 m | | |
| 0.5 m | | |

# Glossary

**acceleration**—rate of change of velocity; speeding up

**binomial theorem**—method used for finding the sum of a mathematical series

**calculus**—method of calculating a quantity from other known quantities that it is related to; for example, velocity from acceleration; a type of math

**drag**—the force that acts against the movement of an object

**escape velocity**—velocity needed to escape the gravitational field of a body

**force**—push or pull that usually makes things move

**gravity**—attractive force that acts on mass

**inertia**—resistance to a change in motion

**mass**—amount of matter

**mathematician**—person who works with mathematics

**newton**—the standard unit used to measure force

**Newton's Rings**—pattern of light made by putting a high-quality lens on a very smooth piece of flat glass

*Principia*—famous book written by Isaac Newton on the laws of nature

**prism**—solid glass shape used in light experiments

**reflecting microscope**—device that uses mirrors instead of lenses to look at very small things, such as insects

**reflector telescope**—device that uses mirrors instead of lenses to look at objects in the sky, such as stars

**sextant**—device used by sailors to find their position using the height of the sun or stars as guidelines

**spectrum**—rainbow of colors that make up white light

**white light**—light that appears colorless but is made up of all the colors of the spectrum—for example, sunlight

# Index

# Sally Ride Science

Sally Ride Science™ is an innovative content company dedicated to fueling young people's interests in science. Our publications and programs provide opportunities for students and teachers to explore the captivating world of science—from astrobiology to zoology. We bring science to life and show young people that science is creative, collaborative, fascinating, and fun.

# Image Credits

Cover Christie's Images/SuperStock; p.3 Liv Falvey/Shutterstock; p.4 (top) Lexy Sinnott/Shutterstock; p.4 (left) The Granger Collection, New York; p.4 (right) Christie's Images /SuperStock; p.5 (back) Elena Elisseeva/Shutterstock; p.5 (top) Mary Evans Picture Library/Alamy; p.5 (bottom) Chris Kryzanek/iStockphoto.com; p.6 (top) Elmtree Images/Alamy; p. 6 (bottom)Dhoxax/Shutterstock; p.7 (right) Duncan Walke/iStockphoto; p.7 (left) The Granger Collection, New York; p.8 (top) The Granger Collection, New York; p.8 (bottom) ErickN/Shutterstock; p.9 (right) Library of Congress; p.9 (left) Photos.com; p.10 (top) Photos.com; p.10 (bottom) Diego Cervo/Shutterstock; p.10–11 Photos.com; p.11 Margaret Smeaton/Shutterstock; p.12 (top) The Granger Collection, New York; p.12 (bottom) Photos.com; p.13 (left) Photos.com; p.13 (right) The Granger Collection, New York; p.14 Jeff Hinds/Shutterstock; p.15 Jason Lugo/iStockphoto.com; p.16 (top) Chris Harvey/Shutterstock; p.16 (bottom) Photos.com; p.17 (left) Jan Kaliciak/Shutterstock; p.17 (right) The Granger Collection, New York; p.18 Peter Baxter/Shutterstock; p.19 Photos.com; p.20 (top) Photos.com; p.20 (bottom) Stijn Peeters/Shutterstock; p.21 The Granger Collection, New York; p.22 (top) Photos.com; p.22 (bottom, right) Photo Researchers Inc., New York; p.22–23 (bottom, left) Photo Researchers, Inc. ; p.23 (left) Photos.com; p.23 (right) Tim Bradley; p.25 (top) The Granger Collection, New York; p.25 (bottom) The Granger Collection, New York; p26 (back) Cary Kalscheuer/Shutterstock; p.26 (bottom) Walt Disney World; p.26–27 Kenneth Denton; p.27 Michael Braun/iStockphoto.com; p.28 (top) Photos.com; p.28–29 Nicoll Rager Fuller; p.32 Getty Images